AMAZING ANIMALS

Sharks

Stacy Tornio

muddy boots™

we jump in puddles

Lanham · Boulder · New York · London

Published by Muddy Boots
An Imprint of Globe Pequot
The Rowman & LIttlefield Publishing Group
4501 Forbes Boulevard, Suite 200, Lanham, Maryland 20706
www.rowman.com

Unit A, Whitacre Mews, 26-34 Stannary Street, London, SE11 4AB

Distributed by NATIONAL BOOK NETWORK

© 2018 The National Wildlife Federation. All rights reserved.

Book design by Katie Jennings Design

Photo credits: p. 1 James Peddle/NWF; p. 3 Leighton Lum/NWF; p. 4 CreativeCommons image; p. 5 (top) AP Images/iStock and (bottom) Divepic/iStock; p. 7 Violetastock/iStock; p. 8 and 9 Global_Pics/ GettyImages; p. 10 Becca Saunders/Minden Pictures; p. 11 frameyazoo/iStock; p. 12 Tony Wu/Minden Pictures; p. 13 Ryo Sato/Flikr; p. 14 (top) Doctor Bass/iStock and (bottom) Rick Starr/NOAA; p. 15 NOAA OKEANOS Explorer Program/Flickr; p. 16 (top) SeaPics.com and (bottom) HeartyPanther/ Flickr; p. 17 Elizabeth Hoffman/iStock; p. 18 Matt Potenski/GettyImages; p. 19 (top) iStock and (bottom) Jeffrey Rotman/Minden Pictures; p. 20 (top) Velvetfish/iStock and (bottom) Leighton Lum/NWF; p. 21 (left) Divepic/iStock and (right) Placebo365/iStock; p. 22 Varga Jones/iStock; p. 23 Kgrif/iStock; p. 24 (top) SeaPics.com and (bottom) SeaPics.com; p. 25 Doug Perrine/Minden Pictures; p. 26 (top) iStock and (bottom) MagicColors/GettyImages; p. 27 Divepic/iStock; p. 28 Rasmus Raahauge/iStock; p. 29 barbaraaaa/iStock; p. 30 (top) Connah/iStock and (bottom) SeaPics.com; p. 31 PetesPhotography/ iStock; p. 32 McClureMr/iStock; p. 33 Laraish/iStock; p. 34 NaluPhoto/iStock; p. 35 (top) Juniper Creek and (bottom) SeaPics.com; p. 36 Kcollie/iStock, p. 38 USACE and George Jumara/iStock; p. 39 iStock

The National Wildlife Federation & Ranger Rick contributors: Children's Publication Staff, Licensing Staff including Deana Duffek, Michael Morris, and Kristen Ferriere, and the National Wildlife Federation in-house naturalist, David Mizejewski.

Thank you for joining the National Wildlife Federation and Muddy Boots in preserving endangered animals and protecting vital wildlife habitats. The National Wildlife Federation is a voice for wildlife protection, dedicated to preserving America's outdoor traditions and inspiring generations of conservationists.

Library of Congress Cataloging-in-Publication Data Available

ISBN 978-1-63076-288-9 (paperback)

ISBN 978-1-63076-289-6 (e-book)

Sharks are some of the most popular and loved creatures in the entire ocean. There are many different kinds of sharks. Some are large and others are small, but all sharks are intelligent animals with special adaptations that help them survive in the ocean. Unfortunately, sharks have a bad reputation as scary, dangerous monsters. But don't believe everything you see on TV or in the movies. It's time to set some of those records straight once and for all! Let's start learning about these amazing ocean animals.

Reef shark

As with all wildlife, you want to give sharks, like the reef shark above, their space. You can still respect them from a distance.

THE BASICS OF SHARKS

When most people think of sharks, they picture the great white shark, which is the same one featured in the movie *Jaws*. Yikes—you should stay away, right? Well, it's always a good idea to give wildlife lots of space, but don't fear them. While it's true that great white sharks are some of the top predators in the ocean—hunting seals, sea lions, squid, and fish—including other sharks. They don't really go after people like many movies portray. In fact, if they do bite a swimmer or surfer, there's a good chance they mistook them for another sea animal.

The bottom line is, you shouldn't think of sharks as killers or scary creatures. There are 400+ other species of sharks in the ocean to learn about. Plus, most of them aren't even very big. Yep, forget about those visions of huge, scary sharks. Only 20% of sharks are larger than an average size man!

As you're learning about sharks, it's important to remember that they can vary a great deal from one to the next. However, before we learn about some of those cool differences, let's take a look at the things most sharks have in common.

The great white shark is a skilled hunter

WHAT MAKES A SHARK A SHARK?

FIRST OF ALL, SHARKS DON'T REALLY HAVE BONES like most animals. Instead, their skeletons are made up of cartilage. This is the same kind of material you'd find in human noses or ears—kind of tough and rubbery. Since cartilage is lighter and more flexible than bones, it helps the sharks maneuver through the water with ease.

Next up, let's look at fins. Most sharks also have a distinct dorsal fin. This is the fin that sticks up in a triangular shape around the middle of the body. If you want to take your fin knowledge to the next level, there are a couple of other terms you can learn. The pectoral fins of a shark are along the bottom. (Think of these as a shark's arms.) Then the caudal fin (also called the tail fin) is in the back. All of these fins can vary from one shark to the next, but keep an eye out for them when comparing different species.

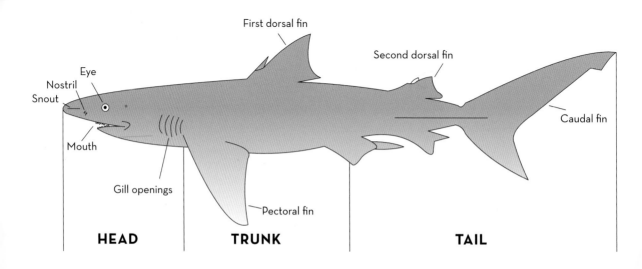

First dorsal fin

Second dorsal fin

Eye

Nostril

Snout

Caudal fin

Mouth

Gill openings

Pectoral fin

HEAD   **TRUNK**   **TAIL**

A shark dorsal fins breaks the water.

Another thing all sharks have in common is gills! Most have five gill slits, though a handful of sharks might have six or seven. No matter the number, the gills serve a very important purpose. When a shark sucks water in through its mouth, the water passes over the gills. The oxygen in the water is absorbed into the shark's blood vessels through the gills, and carbon dioxide from the shark's blood stream exits into the water. This is how gills help a shark breathe.

The five gills are easily visible on this lemon shark.

Sharks are also famous for their teeth. Their jaws have many rows of teeth and a single shark can grow thousands of teeth in its lifetime. Can you imagine having to brush all those teeth?

One popular myth about sharks is that they can detect a single drop of blood in the water from miles away. This isn't true, but sharks do have an acute sense of smell thanks to its sensitive receptors. A shark's nostrils, located on the bottom of its snout, are lined with special cells that can pick up tiny amounts of dissolved chemicals (like blood) in the water that passes through their nose! This helps the shark hunt prey and locate members of the opposite sex for breeding.

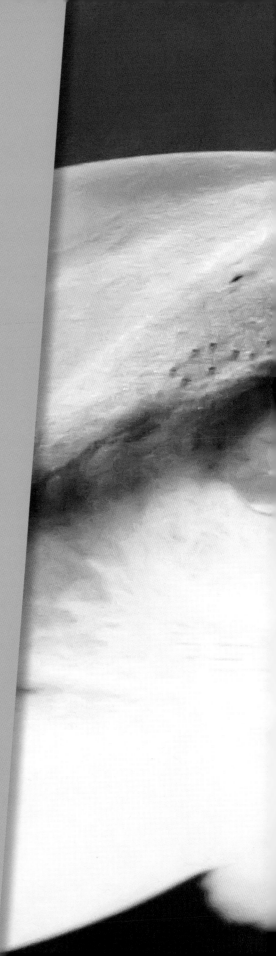

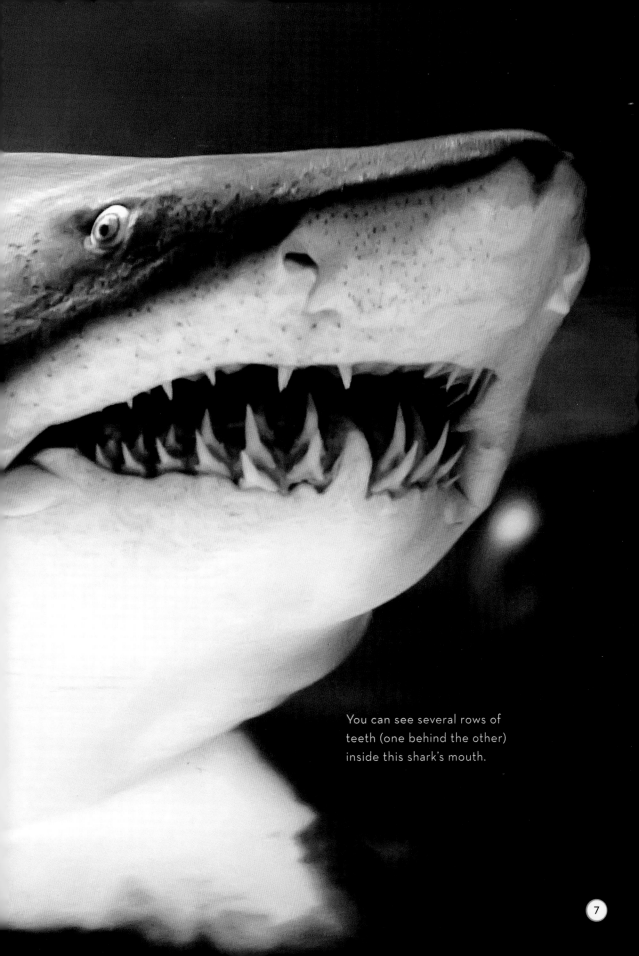

You can see several rows of teeth (one behind the other) inside this shark's mouth.

It can be very dark in the ocean, so a shark depends on its sense of smell to find food. Sharks also have additional senses that people don't have in order to detect the movements of other animals underwater. A shark's head and snout are covered with several thousand small pores (called ampullae of Lorenzini) that connect to nerves below the skin. The muscle movements of fish and other sea creatures create electrical signals that are picked up by the shark's ampullae and then signal the shark's brain that food is near. Sharks can also use their electric pulse detecting pores like a GPS to navigate through the water. A shark also has a feature called a lateral line that extends from its head down its body. The lateral line is used to detect vibrations and changes in pressure caused by currents or other animals.

Sharks come in all shapes and sizes, but they share common features, such as skeletons made of cartilage, fins, gills, lots of teeth, and additional senses for hunting prey and navigating the dark ocean waters. Now that you know a little bit more about sharks, let's dive into the different ways that sharks are divided in the animal world. There are eight main classifications, which scientists call orders. Let's take a closer look.

This grey reef shark uses its ampullae and lateral line to sense the movements and location of food swimming nearby.

The sawshark has a long, sword-like snout that helps It hunt its prey in the sandy ocean bottom.

A sawfish (pictured left) looks similar to a sawshark, but it is actually a type of ray. Rays are closely related to sharks.

The Sawsharks

At first glance, sawsharks don't look like a typical shark, but behind the strange appearance, they have all the characteristics of a shark—a cartilage skeleton, fins, gills, and teeth. They are named for the long snouts coming out the front of their heads like a sword. These snouts are edged with sharp teeth and serve an important purpose. The sharks will hover at the bottom of the ocean floor and use their snout to sense fish, crustaceans, and squid that might be hiding in the sand. Then they will use their snouts to kill their prey and occasionally cut it into smaller pieces that can be easily swallowed. After that, it's ready to eat. It's a good thing it has this tool because the mouths of sawsharks are relatively small compared to their bodies. You can find nine species of sawsharks in the world, including the longnose, shortnose, sixgill, and eastern sawshark. Depending on species, they can grow up to five feet long.

The Angel Sharks

An angel shark has a flat, pancake-like shape. This doesn't seem very shark-like in shape, right? It's long, wide side fins look like wings, which is how it got its name. The eyes of these sharks are on top of their heads, and their gills are on the bottom of their bodies. This is another group of sharks that spend most of their time along the bottom of the ocean. Their flat bodies help them hide in the sand or murky water, waiting for prey, including fish, crustaceans, and mollusks. When anything tasty comes near, they will pop out, stretch open their mouths, and snatch their next meal!

Twenty-one species of angel sharks exist in the world. They will eat small fish, crustaceans, snails, and mollusks.

The Lesser Spotted Dogfish is one of the smaller sharks in the dogfish group.

A spiny dogfish shark circles the ocean floor looking for his next meal.

The Dogfish Sharks

This shark group is very large, with 119 species total. Even within this, you can find seven different types, including gulper, sleeper, and lantern sharks. It's really not as confusing as it sounds. This is just a BIG group! Remember this with the dogfish sharks—there are a lot of them so they can vary a lot from one to the next. For instance, the tiny dwarf lantern shark is only six inches long. By comparison, Greenland sharks can get to be more than 20 feet. Most like to be thousands and thousands of feet deep into the ocean.

All the sharks in the dogfish group have two dorsal (back) fins, five gill slits, and give birth to live babies, not eggs.

Greenland sharks (pictured above) are the largest species in the dogfish shark group.

More About Dogfish Sharks

Several of the species in this group have a good trick called bioluminescence. This means they have the ability to glow in the dark using chemicals in their bodies. They will often use this glowing light to lure in prey before they eat them! Some of the common species in this group include the spiny dogfish, gulper shark, birdbeak dogfish, green lanternshark, cookiecutter shark, and needle dogfish. Depending on the size, these sharks will eat all sizes of fish, crustaceans, and even marine mammals in some cases.

Deep under the ocean, this pygmy shark glows in the dark, thanks to bioluminescence.

The spiny dogfish is another member of the dogfish shark group.

A great white shark leaps out of the water to catch its prey.

The Mackerel Sharks

There are only 15 species in this shark group, but it also holds some of the most famous, including the great white shark, the shortfin and longfin makos, the crocodile shark, and the goblin shark.

Most of the species in this group have a long body, snout, and prominent dorsal fins. Their head shapes are also very similar with eyes on the tops of their heads and their mouths underneath. These sharks vary a great deal in size. The crocodile shark is only 3 feet long, and the basking shark is more than 30 feet long. When people think of sharks, swimming along the top of the ocean, chances are they are imagining sharks in this family. It's true that several of these species will hang out near the surface of the water, but this is definitely not the case for all. For example, goblin sharks are part of this group, and they hang out in depths of 100 to nearly 1,000 feet! The goblin shark's paddle-shaped snout has special sensors that can pick up electrical currents. All living things give off these currents, so the sensors help the shark find squid, fish, crabs, and other prey.

A shortfin mako shark swims below the ocean's surface.

More About Mackerel Sharks

Crocodile sharks are another mackerel species that stays along the bottom of the ocean up to 2,000 feet deep. In fact, they live so far down that scientists are still trying to learn about them—they are a bit of a mystery!

When it comes to food, most of the sharks in this group will eat fish, squid, and other marine animals, but it's important to note that two—the basking sharks and the megamouth sharks—are plankton eaters. Plankton are tiny organisms that live in the ocean.

It's diversity like this that makes studying sharks so interesting!

The goblin shark has a very different appearance than the typical shark.

The basking shark and megamouth shark use their large mouths to feed on plankton.

The tasseled wobbegong blends in with the reef.
Pretty impressive camouflage!

A whale shark is a gentle visitor to this kayaker.

The Carpet Sharks

Think about the name of this group for a moment—carpet sharks. Why would they have a name like this? This group often hangs out near the ocean floor or in shallow water. Many are flat, too, blending into their surroundings much like a piece of carpet.

The tasseled wobbegong is named for the flaps and fringes that make it look more like a shag rug than an ocean predator.

The only exception to this rule in the carpet shark group is the whale shark, which hangs out at the top of the water and eats plankton. The whale shark is also the largest known fish in the world; it can grow to more than 40 feet long and weigh 20 tons!

Others in this group will eat fish, sea urchins, crabs, shrimp and other sea creatures.

Carpet sharks like warm waters, and nearly all in this group are in the Indo-Pacific area, which includes the tropical waters of the Indian Ocean and warm areas of the Pacific Ocean (so mostly the central and western areas). You can find 39 species in this group, including the hooded carpet shark, nurse shark, spotted wobbegong, blind shark, and the popular leopard shark.

The leopard shark gets its name from its spotted skin.

A nurse shark swims along the reef.

The Bullhead Sharks

If you think of most sharks as being stealthy, swift, and even graceful, then you might have to change your definition with bullhead sharks. They have kind of awkward, oversized heads, and their movements are a little bit like this, too. While many sharks have elongated snouts, the snouts of bullhead sharks are kind of stubby instead.

These sharks are usually 2 to 6 feet in size, and often hang out in waters around 300 feet deep. They tend to eat all types of crustaceans and small fish. They might not be the most famous sharks out there, but they are still cool. You can find 9 species total, including zebra bullhead shark, horn shark, and crested bullhead shark.

The Galapagos bullhead shark hunts for crabs and small fish along the rocky ocean bottom.

This horn shark is not as graceful as its larger shark cousins.

The Cow Sharks

In a lot of ways, the four species in this group are some of the most mysterious of all sharks. This is because most of their time is spent in the deep, dark, cold waters of the ocean. Some scientists classify this group as the sixgilled sharks since the majority of the species have six pairs of gills, compared to most sharks that only have five. Of course, there always seems to be an exception to the rule. In this case, some cow sharks have seven sets of gills!

When it's time for cow sharks to give birth, many come up to the surface of the water and have as many as 80 babies—called pups! These large sharks range between 4 and 15 feet, and they're not afraid to go after large prey, including other sharks, seals, rays, and big and small fish. Two of the most well-known sharks in this group include the sharpnose sevengill shark and the bluntnose sixgill shark.

Broadnose sevengill sharks, or cow sharks, spend most of their lives in the deepest parts of the ocean.

The sharpnose sevengill shark is one of the most well known in the cow shark group.

A spotted cow shark
swims around a reef.

A blue shark swims close to the water's surface.

The unique shape of the hammerhead shark's head allows it to see in many directions (up, down, left, right) at the same time.

The Ground Sharks

Today, this is the largest group of sharks with 277 different species, but you never know when science will reclassify the groups, or perhaps a new discovery will be made! Even though there are a lot of different types of ground sharks, they all share a similar, slender body shape about 2 to 3 feet long (though some grow up to 10 feet).

Most have an elongated snout, too, except for the hammerheads—they have flat, almost triangular-shaped heads. Some ground sharks go deep into the ocean while others stay in shallower areas.

You might see them swimming in the open ocean or along the coasts. They're also common in the Atlantic, Pacific, and Indian Oceans. The sharks in this group are considered generalists as far as food goes, meaning they will eat just about anything from fish, squid, snakes, rays, and even other sharks.

Within this huge group, you'll find 8 species in the hammerhead sharks group; 54 species in the whaler sharks group, which includes tiger sharks and blue sharks; 47 species in the smoothhound sharks group, including the longnose houndshark; and 150 different species of catsharks including the ghost catshark.

This tiger shark swims through shallow waters.

THE TRUTH ABOUT SHARKS

THERE IS A LOT OF MISINFORMATION OUT THERE ABOUT SHARKS, and believing the myths about these amazing animals can be dangerous—for you and the sharks! In the following section we will separate fact from fiction.

MYTH: All sharks are dangerous.

TRUTH: Less than one percent of shark species are dangerous to people. You have a better chance of getting struck by lightning than to have a shark encounter. It might seem hard to believe, but it's true. Shark species that occasionally do bite people, such as the great white shark or the bull shark, tend to give a lot of sharks a bad reputation. The truth is that most species are not potentially dangerous to people, and sharks rarely seek out people to attack them. Usually a shark bite happens as a result of mistaken identity when a shark thinks a swimmer is another shark or a seal. In fact, scientists who study sharks encourage others NOT to use the term "shark attack."

Great white sharks like this one sometimes bite swimmers when they mistake people for other prey.

Leopard sharks hunt in kelp forests that grow at the bottom of the ocean.

MYTH: There are only a few species of sharks in the world.

TRUTH: You can find more than 450 species of sharks in the world, but this number could go up at any time. As scientists get better at studying the ocean and the creatures that live deep in the waters, they actually discover new species. So you never know when you might hear about a newly discovered shark! Cool huh?

A group of Blacktip reef sharks hunts for fish in the shallow waters.

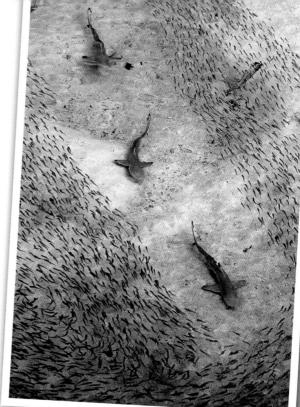

MYTH: Sharks swim near the top of water—you can often see their fins.

TRUTH: It might be hard to get that triangle fin image out of your mind because you've probably seen movies or pictures of this. But you should know that most sharks don't hunt that close to the surface of the water. Sharks are found in every level of the ocean. In addition, they rarely expose their dorsal fin above the water, even though this is what you see in the movies. There are so many sharks in the world, and many of them are found in mid to deep ocean waters.

A horn shark feeds on squid eggs on the ocean floor.

Despite its large size, a whale shark eats mostly plankton.

MYTH: All sharks feed on fish, seals, and dolphins.

TRUTH: Sharks eat a variety of foods—some sharks don't eat animals at all, but most shark species feed on things like fish, crustaceans, and squid. These sharks eat plankton, which are small, microscopic organisms that float through the ocean. In fact, the largest shark in the world—the whale shark—is a plankton eater. Other sharks might go after some larger marine mammals, like sea lions and dolphins, if they can find them. But most of the time their diet is made up of fish, lobsters, crabs, and squid.

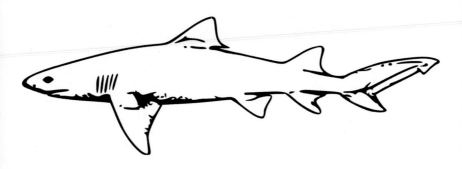

MYTH: All sharks have sharp, pointy, scary teeth.

TRUTH: There are four different types of shark teeth that vary in size and shape, depending on the kinds of food that shark species eats. While people have several different kinds of teeth within their mouths, each shark species has only one kind of tooth throughout its mouth—and a lot of them!

Each shark species has teeth specially designed for the kind of food they eat. Most people likely think of the great white shark's teeth, which are triangular, with sharp and jagged edges. Since most of their food is other large marine creatures, they need to be able to use their teeth to shred their prey.

But some sharks have long and thin, needle-like teeth, which are often used for gripping slippery food. Other sharks have flat, plate-like teeth that are used for crushing their prey. And finally, you have the teeth of the plankton eaters.

Like the great white shark, a tiger shark's teeth have jagged edges that help it tear into and grip its prey.

The jaw of a great white shark shows the multiple rows of teeth.

The whale shark is a plankton eater, and its teeth are small and insignificant. They don't need to use their teeth to grip, grind, or slice their food because the plankton they eat are already very tiny.

Here's one thing that nearly all sharks have in common about their teeth, though. They have multiple rows, and they tend to lose and grow hundreds of new teeth during their lifetime.

When one tooth is lost, another from a back row will move in to take its place. This is weird to think about, right? How does that work? Well it's possible because the teeth are not embedded into the jaw as human teeth are. They are attached to the skin, making them easier to be mobile.

This tiger shark uses his nostrils for smelling, not breathing.

MYTH: Sharks can smell a drop of blood from miles away.

TRUTH: This one is tricky because sharks do have a very good sense of smell. In fact, it's better than a lot of other animals. But miles away might be a bit of an exaggeration. Scientists estimate that some species of predatory shark can smell potential prey nearly a quarter of a mile—still pretty impressive, though! Sharks' nostrils don't have anything to do with breathing, and they aren't near the mouth. They are on the underside of sharks' snouts.

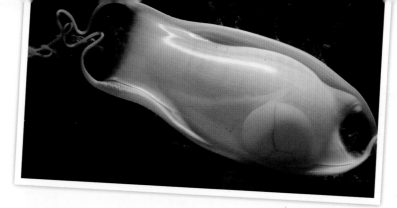

MYTH: All sharks lay eggs.

TRUTH: It's a mix. Some sharks lay eggs while others give birth to their young. There are scientific names for these different ways of bearing young. The egg-laying shark species are called **oviparous**, while those that give live birth are called **oviviparous**. An egg-laying shark will create a leathery case, sometimes called a "mermaid's purse," (see picture above) with a yolk sac inside that keeps the baby shark fed as it grows. Regardless of whether they are born live or hatch from an egg, baby sharks (called pups) have to learn to survive on their own because sharks do not stick around to care for their young as many mammals do.

So how do the numbers break down? About 60 percent of all sharks fall into the live birth category. In this case, the pups actually have a better long-term chance of survival.

This mother lemon shark gives birth to her pups in a shallow lagoon before swimming away.

Sharks are beautiful creatures that deserve our protection. Here, a white-tipped reef shark emerges from a cave.

MYTH: Shark populations are doing great!

TRUTH: Overall shark populations are declining—by a lot! In a study of eight shark species during the past 15 years, scientists found that the populations declined by as much as half or more! Another report suggests as many as one-third of all sharks and rays (a close shark relative) could be considered endangered, threatened, or vulnerable in the future.

Why is this? Researchers estimate that more than 100 million sharks die in fishing nets or are hunted and killed each year. Some people are hunting them for food while others hunt them just for the sport of it. This is not good news because sharks are an important part of the ocean. We need them in our waters to help keep everything else in order.

MYTH: You can't do anything to help sharks.

TRUTH: While you can't directly stop people from hunting sharks or eating them, you can do your part in other ways. Keep reading to learn how!

MORE ABOUT CONSERVATION STATUS

Conservation status is a ranking system that scientists use to describe the relative number of a species that still exist.

. . . .

Endangered means a species is almost gone or extinct.

. . . .

Threatened species are on their way to becoming endangered through hunting or habitat loss.

. . . .

Many shark species are **vulnerable** to becoming threatened or endangered if we don't protect them.

HOW YOU CAN HELP

A group of students study a shark's jaw bone in a presentation by the U.S. Army Corps of Engineers on ocean preservation. Look at all those teeth!

1. You've already taken the first step by educating yourself about sharks. Now you can teach your friends and family members about the important role that sharks play in maintaining a healthy ocean. The more people understand about these amazing animals, the easier it is to make choices that protect shark species.

2. Make better buying decisions with your family by not purchasing or using beauty products (such as makeup) containing Squalene (shark liver oil). Read the ingredients on the labels of all your products before you buy and choose cruelty-free products instead.

3. Defend sharks by speaking out. If you see anyone abusing sharks or doing something that could endanger these incredible and valuable creatures, always report them to the proper authorities.

4. Ask your parents to help you write a letter to your local senator, congressman, or even your favorite celebrity, to inform them about what is going on with our oceans. Ask this person to use his or her voice and influence to help bring an end to shark finning and protect our ocean's sharks. You could also ask your teacher to help you get your classmates involved in a letter-writing campaign to save the sharks!

5. There are hundreds of organizations all over the world working every day to save sharks, including Project AWARE, Shark Savers, and the Shark Research Institute. Choose an organization (local, national, non-profit) close to your hometown and contact it to learn more about how you can help protect the world's oceans and save sharks no matter where you live. You could volunteer your time or hold a fundraiser to help pay for its important work.